Me Without You

"Healing Hearts" Series

Written by

Janice Jobey

Dedicated to the memory of my beautiful Grandmother, Lora Inez, who lives in my heart and who gave me the gift of kindness and love.

Copyright 2017

Early Learning Innovations, LLC

Bringing Life to Early Childhood

Copyright 2017

Early Learning Innovations, LLC

This book provides an opportunity to talk about feelings of losing a loved one. Sad, lonely, and lost are some of the feelings a child might have. Being able to express feelings can be difficult and helping them find words and ways to express what they're feeling can be healing.

Additionally, this book illustrates simple ways to keep the loved one alive inside. Opportunities to have meaningful conversations abound throughout the book.

Look for more books in the "Healing Hearts" series to come--divorce, grief and loss, children separated by incarcerated parents, and other topics.

Copyright 2017

Early Learning Innovations, LLC

Bringing Life to Early Childhood

Get Ready to read "Me Without You"!

* Be sure to also read our companion book, "Some Day"!

* Don't feel the need to read through the whole book...a page or two at a time can be sufficient considering the deep emotional aspect of this topic.

* The **Conversational Extenders** at the bottom of each spread, provide meaningful communication support for those assisting children in talking about feelings and ways to heal. Please personalize "loved one" with the name of your "loved one".

* **GET READY!** Have a notebook and pen and write down the answers to the questions on the Conversational Extenders! You might use a child's responses to help them write a book about their feelings. Encourage the child to illustrate it.

* Read the section in the back of the book about **"Talking to Children about Death"**. These are suggestions ONLY, as there are many ways to approach the topic of death and are meant only to support you in this topic. Every family will have their own traditions, strengths, coping mechanisms, and resources that should also be used.

* Be ready to provide vocabulary for feelings. The concrete analogies will help define and expand this discussion. Discuss the "pumping heart" and the "feeling heart" and while the same, they are different. The "pumping heart" may actually feel the hurt of the "feeling heart". "Heart" can be spoken of in the physical sense as well as in the emotional sense.

* While this book is NOT a substitute for mental health services that may also be beneficial to a child suffering a loss, it may be helpful in opening up discussion and helping the child to realize that talking about the loved one is healthy.

Conversational Extenders:

* What do you think this book is about?   Why?

* What do you think the title means?

* Who do you like to be "with"?

Like a dove without a coo,

Like a cow without her moo,

Like a room without a view.

That's how I feel ...
Me without you!

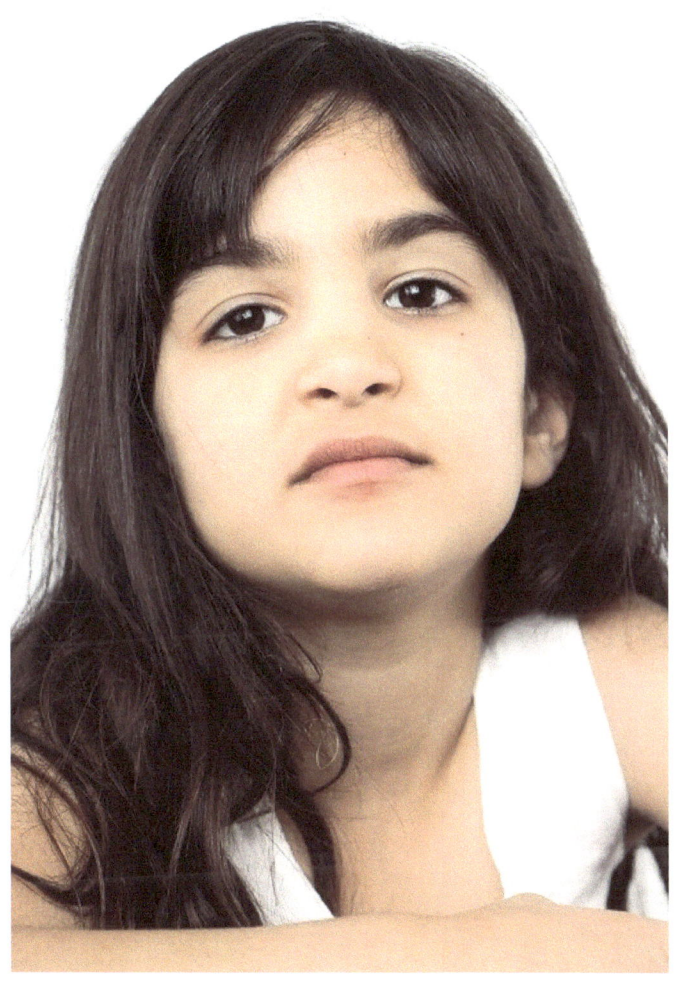

Conversational Extenders:

*   What are some words to describe how it feels to no longer be able to see your loved one (use name of person to personalize)? How do you think this girl is feeling in this picture?

* Does your sadness make you quiet sometimes? Like the dove or the cow? Are they still a dove and a cow even if they make no sound? It's okay to not talk but it's also good if you can talk to someone about your feelings. Who could you talk to?

* How do you think it might feel to be in a room where you couldn't see out? Have you ever felt like that?

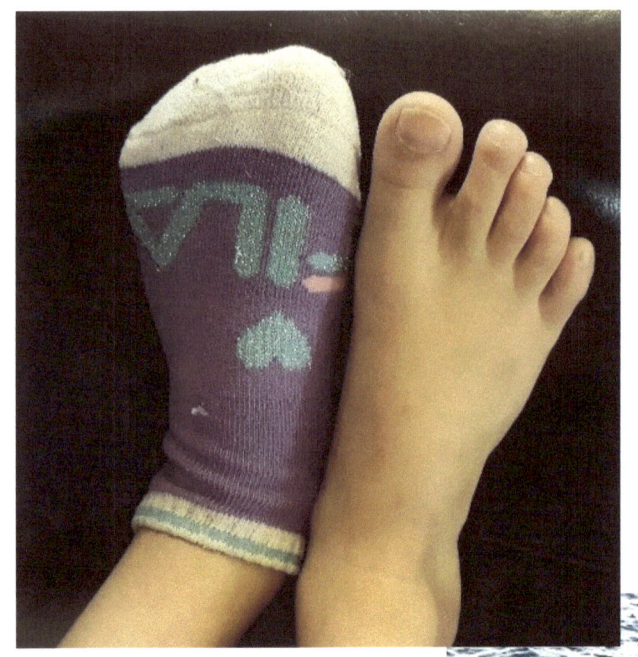

Like a foot without a sock,

Like a boat without a dock.

Like a clock without a tock.

That's how it feels...
Me Without You.

But, when you're feeling your loss, Pictures can be like roses in moss.

Conversational Extenders:

*   Discuss things that "go-together" like on the previous page. When something is "missing" is that item still that item (is a clock still a clock even without a tock)? How did it feel to be *with* your loved one? Without?

*   How do pictures help when we miss someone? Do you have pictures of you with your loved one? What might you do with your pictures so that you can keep your loved one close?

Like a garden without a bee,

Like a bird without a tree,

Like a lock without a key,

That's how it feels...
Me Without You.

But, when you're feeling sad, Memories are like a lily on a pad.

Conversational Extenders:

*   Why are bees good for gardens? Why do some birds need trees? Why do you need a key for a lock? (Those things function better when they are together). How did your loved one help you? What did they do for you? Who can help you do those things now?

*   What memories do you have with your loved one? What were your loved ones favorite things to do? To eat? Favorite color?

*   Do you think that lily pad would be just as pretty without the lily flower? How can memories of our loved one make our life better?

Like a knife and fork without a spoon,

Like the stars without a moon,

Like a song without a tune,

That's how it feels... Me Without You.

But sharing a story about you, will put
The sun back in the sky.

Conversational Extenders:

* Do you need a spoon to eat? Can you eat soup with a fork and knife?

* How does the moon help you to see the stars at night?

* How does "Itsy Bitsy Spider" sound if we speak rather than sing it? Try it. How does it sound?

* How do some things (or people) help us do certain things better? Did your loved one help you do things better? Who can help you now?

* Can you tell a story about something you and your loved one did? How does telling stories allow our loved one to live on in our hearts?

Like a head without a hat,

Like a ball without a bat,

Like a kitten without a cat,

That's how it feels...
Me Without You.

But, mementos are like the swim in the swan.

Conversational Extenders:

* Why does a kitten need a cat? Why does a baseball need a bat? How does it feel for your body to be warm but your head cold? How is this like being without your loved one?

* What are mementos? It is an "keepsake". It helps us remember a person, a place, or an event. It could be a special gift that your loved one gave you or something you have from a trip to the zoo or park. What mementos do you have from your loved one? How do mementos help us keep our loved one in our heart?

* Do you think swans like to swim? How does this swan being able to swim make it beautiful? Mementos can be beautiful too.

Like a present without a bow,

Like cold without snow,

Like a bell without a cow,

That's how it feels...
Me Without You.

Things might not seem as bright But memories are like the shine in the light.

Conversational Extenders:

* If you get a present and it doesn't have a bow on it, is it still a present? If you have a cowbell hanging on your door, does it mean it's not a cowbell? Can you have cold without snow? Are you still "you" even if your loved one is gone? How can you keep your loved one with you?

* What are memories? What memories do you have with your loved one? How can memories make our day "shinier/brighter?

Like stripes on a zebra,

Like scales on an iguana,

Like hair on a gorilla,

That's how we are...
Me and You.

The sorrow may not go away, But little joys will be like the song of a blue jay.

Conversational Extenders:

* Can a person take the stripes off a zebra? Or the scales off an iguana? Or the hair off a gorilla? NO! Can another person take the memories of your loved one from you? Can another person take your sadness away?

* How do you think a blue jay sounds? Happy? What are some things that you can do that make you happy. Why should we try to be happy even though we may miss our loved one?

Like spots on a butterfly,

Like clouds in blue sky,

Like meringue on pie,

That's how we are...
Me and You.

Finding love with others
Will be like paint on paper.

Conversational Extenders:

*   Is a butterfly still a butterfly whether it has spots or not? Is the sky still blue with or without clouds? Is it a pie even if it doesn't have meringue on top?

*   Our loved one lived in the world with us at one time. But now, our loved one lives within us. They are still with us, just in different ways.

*   Who else loves us? Who else do we love? How is paint on paper like love from others? Does love from others help up? Brighten your world?

*   Can you paint a picture of how someone you love makes you feel?

Like a light
in the fog,

Like a bark
of a dog,

Like a frog
on a log,

That's how we are...
Me and You.

Your loved one no longer feels pain
And that is like Sunshine in rain.

Conversational Extenders:

*   How do these things on the preceding page "go together"? How did you and your loved one "go together"?

*   Sometimes people are in a great deal of pain because of a condition, disease, or injury. Your loved one may have been in pain. Have you ever had pain? What from? How did it feel? Did that pain go away? What if that pain never went away? How would that make you feel? How does it make you feel to know your loved one will never feel pain again. How is that like "sunshine in rain"? (It may be that their death was good for them even though it was sad for you.)

*   Did you know that the sun shining in the rain makes a rainbow?

Like the warmth of a mug,

Like a bug in a rug,

Like the squeeze of a hug,

That's how we are...
Me and You.

Know that your loved one lives on in you…
Like glitter in glue.

Conversational Extenders:

* How does a warm cup of chocolate or soup make you feel? Do you think a "bug in a rug" is warm? How do hugs make you feel?

* Can you take the glitter out of the glitter glue? Can you take the glue out of the glitter? NO! Can you take your loved one out of your heart? NO! How does it feel to know that your loved lives in your heart and that he/she will always be with you?

Someone you love may have died, But the love you shared is still alive.

Conversational Extenders:

*   What are some things you will do to keep your loved one alive within you?

*   Paint or Draw a picture of how your loved on lives in your heart.

Let your loved one live on in you
And live each day in a way
that their love for you shines through
in all that you do.

Conversational Extenders:

*   Tell me about your loved one? Can you describe them? How did they treat you/others? How did they help others? What were things about them that you liked?

*   Do you think your loved one would want you to be kind and caring toward others? If they "live in your heart", then you can have their help in knowing how to be kind and loving toward others.

Talking to Children About Death

Young children are often touched by death . . . a grandparent, a parent, a neighbor, a distant relative, a pet . . . someone they know dies. Death is a difficult concept for young children to grasp. They begin to question, develop their own ideas and express their feelings in various ways. Losing a close family member is especially difficult. Understanding how children understand death developmentally, can help adults support young children with the loss of a loved one.

Infants and Toddlers are not able to understand death but may respond to the separation of a close caregiver. Maintaining routines and consistent care giving is very important.

Preschoolers are unable to understand that death is a permanent state, so patience and gentle reminders that the loved one is gone but that memories last forever will help. Because they may not have words to express their feelings, thoughts, or fears, you might see behavior expressed in play, behavior, or they might exhibit emotional reactions or physical symptoms.

School-agers can understand death and can think about this concept. However, their understanding may not be accurate. Death might be personified as a "boogey man", or may believe that they are to blame, or fear that they will be left alone. School-agers will need help with expressing their thoughts and fears and gentle support in correcting misconceptions. Children will pick up on how others are handling the loss and will imitate those responses.

Here are some ideas and suggestions that may help loved ones say goodbye or help surviving loved ones to talk to a child about death.

What is Dead?

1. Simple, honest answers are the best. Answer openly and truthfully. Children need answers in terms they can understand. Try this: "When someone is dead, it means they aren't alive. They can't eat, sleep, move, or feel anything."

2. "Going to sleep", "we lost our dad", and similar explanations can cause confusion and fear in the child. Will he die if he goes to sleep? If Daddy "goes away" on a trip, will he die?"

3. A "dead" state is hard for a young child to comprehend. Never to walk again, never to breathe again is an unchanging state.

Where is _____ now?

1. What happens to a person when they die can be confusing to a child. Again a simple answer such as "The body is put in a box and then into a hole in the ground in the cemetery. His name will be on a tombstone in the grave." But your loved one's memories can "live" on in our hearts.

2. Support the child with the family's personal religious beliefs. While answers like "he's gone to heaven" can be confusing to the child, it can be helpful to use concrete terms as discussed in the previous section.

3. Visiting the cemetery or place of interment is a good idea. This allows the child to understand your answers. It's also a way of remembering the one who has died.

Why do people die?

1. A child may ask this after he has thought about death for awhile. "If my grandma died because she 'got sick', then I might die too if I get sick."
2. You can discuss old age, chronic diseases or catastrophic illness, and accidents with your child. Reassure him that just because a person "gets sick" doesn't mean he'll die.

Other ideas that work

1. Allow your child to pretend play about death. This is a child's way of working out fears and answers to questions.

2. Discuss feelings openly and honestly with your child. Accept and acknowledge his feelings whether negative or positive. Also, talk about how you feel. "I was very sad when grandma died. I miss her a lot. You look sad too." A child may need to talk about this often.

3. Let the child tell a story about the person who has died. Write it down for him.

4. Visit the cemetery, take flowers, and talk openly and honestly about his death.

5. Answer questions simply. If and when he wants more detail, he'll ask more questions.

6. Make a memory book, compiling memories and photos.

Death is a natural occurrence in life just as birth is. Remember to let the child learn in his way . . . by seeing, doing and touching.

Copyright 2017 Early Learning Innovations, LLC

About the Author
Janice S. Jobey, M.S., M.S., CCPS

Janice Jobey is an early childhood expert specializing in literacy, learning, and mental health. Her own childhood experiences with hearing and speech challenges has provided passion in promoting phonological awareness in young children through everyday experiences. Her vast experiences from childhood to "grand-mother-hood" provide the basis for her books and energetic speaking engagements. Janice writes curriculum for infants, toddlers, preschoolers, and parent engagement. Her 35 years of teaching experience spans from infants to adults and working with children with special needs. She holds graduate degrees in child development and education. She lives in rural Oklahoma where she enjoys writing books and curriculum, spending time in her gardens, and playing with her grandchildren.

Contact Janice Jobey, M.S., M.S., CCPS

janjobey@gmail.com

www.earlylearning.today

Copyright 2017 Early Learning Innovations, LLC

Other Titles by Janice Jobey

Me: Learning and Growing

Soft to Touch

My Senses

Family Love

Oh Grana!

Oh Poppa!

Snug as a Bug

Dancing On Daddy's Shoes

Rocking in Mama's Arms

Woodland Wonder

Woodland Riddles

Woodland ABC's

Fox in the City

Pet Set

Pet ABCs

Pet Riddles

Pig Prince

Pet Shop

Spring Set

Flower Garden ABC

Spring Shorts

Spring Senses

Me and You

Rules Keep Us Safe

Just Look at My Face

Pretend Fun

A Princess Needs a Crown

Healing Hearts

These 3 Things

Some Day

Me Without You

Healthy Me

Eat The Rainbow

And many more!